CORONAWORLD

CORONAWORLD

Graham Fulton

PENNILESS PRESS PUBLICATIONS
www.pennilesspress.co.uk

First published August 2020

ISBN 978-1-913144-19-7

OTHER BOOKS BY GRAHAM FULTON

Poetry

Humouring the Iron Bar Man
Knights of the Lower Floors
Open Plan
Full Scottish Breakfast
Reclaimed Land
One Day in the Life of Jimmy Denisovich
Pub Dogs of Glasgow (with Reuben Paris)
Photographing Ghosts
Continue
Edible Transmitters
Pub Dogs of London (with Fiona Freund)
Pub Dogs of Manchester (with Georgie Glass)
Brian Wilson in Swansea Bus Station
Paragraphs at the End of the World
Equal Night
Circulation
Something Good Will Always Happen
Flesh and Stone
Glitches of Mortality
Consumption: Selected Pamphlets 2008-2019

Non-Fiction

The Paisley Civil War

some of these poems have appeared in
Poetry from the Backroom:
Hugh McMillan's Pestilence Poems blogspot

the order of the poems in the book
is, with two or three exceptions, the same
as the order in which they were written

front cover photograph
and inside photographs
by Graham Fulton

author photograph
by Helen Nathaniel-Fulton

to Margaret Watson,
and the memory
of David Watson

National Health
March 3 2020

fur fucks sake man
uv jist bin telt
thi coronavirus is on its way
fay China
ur Kilmarnock
thurz gonni bi a lockdown
an road blocks
an firin squads
an makeshift morgz
thurz gonni bi
ut least half a milyin bodies
itll bi like sumthin
oot uv thi walkin deid
wi zombies staggrin
aboot thi streets
crunchin bones
an munchin flesh

am legitimately concernt
fur ma well being

an am no allowt ti sneeze
an am no allowt ti shag
an thur izni enuff
bog roll ti go roun
thurz a shortage
uv Salt & Vinegar crisps
an av bin reliably informed
thur izni enuff soap
um gonni go doon
ti Lidl right now
an demand ma fair share
uv sanitizer
an sanny pads
an corona beer an pizza
fur fucks sake man
ah demand ma human rights

ah demand ti know whit
thi fuck iz goin on
ah need ti bi allowed
ti live ma life wi dignity

07-03-2020
10:31
Hi Jim. Sorry but I reckon
I'm going to have to cancel
my visit to Edinburgh. It's
too risky. You never know who
you're rubbing shoulders with
on the train or on the streets.
I'll see you when we're done
with this thing. I hope
you're keeping okay and
your mum's settling in to
her nursing home. Take care.

the first poets I liked

the ones from school
who wrote about war

Wilfred Owen
Siegfried Sassoon

sad shires
anthems and bells
world-transforming words

cold
mud

normal side by side
with horror

real-
time

kitchen sink chaos
ordinary nightmare

there's a hearse parked
across the road
outside a house

a sleek limousine behind

as the men in black
wait for the mourners
to appear
they're disinfecting
the door handles
and the door that
opens at the back
to let in the coffin

the wreaths
for the loved ones

squirting
wiping
rubbing

making the most
of their vacant time

business is healthy

we're all dragging
the correct bins out
on the correct day
as usual

plastic sizes
blue or grey

it'll be all okay
until the system fails
completely

the unskilled machinery
of society
stops

everyone cowering
in their dark homes

starving
freezing

waiting for civilisation
to burn out
switch off

recycle calendars
little green bags

who will empty
our colourful bins
when this happens?

I take the prescription
for my stay-alive pills
to my doctor's surgery

I have to drop it
into a box held at arm's length
with a woman behind
the counter
looking daggers at me

she's been swabbing
the surface
there's no one else

here we go

next time I expect
there will be
searchlights
tripwires
and minefields
all installed
to keep me out

please go away
expire in private

it's just been announced
by a grim-faced BBC newsreader
that the Eurovision Song Contest
has been cancelled

the cruellest cut of all

flags are being flown
at half-mast all over Europe

filming of *Eastenders*
has also been stopped

life will never be the same again
children are weeping in the streets

in Tesco it's like
World War Two
has been re-declared
although with
a bit less dignity

trolleys are piled high
with paracetamol
and cheesy puffs

frightened pensioners
are expendable
forced to beg for scraps
the items of crap
that nobody else wants

manky sweepings

crying mothers
look for baby milk
but it's all been grabbed
by the family McKnob

food-gangs are shoving
and scrabbling and jostling
for position
as they compete
for the last tin of baked beans
with no added sugar
the last sachet
of microwave porridge

keep Britain the way
it's always been!

only the cruel will prevail

I'm told by the girl
behind the local store counter
that I'm only allowed to buy
one bar of *Dairy Milk*
and one packet
of Salt and Vinegar crisps

I can choose another flavour
if I really need a second packet

alternative flavours
are deemed acceptable
Smoky Bacon or Plain

I only want Salt and Vinegar
which complements
the sweetness of the chocolate

if I go out and come back in
wearing a false moustache
can I buy another?

sitting listening
to what is coming

the soothing sound
of a teatime ambulance

an ice cream van
playing the theme
from *Monty Python*

the schools have been closed
the doors bolted

I'm sure the children
will all be saying
'Oh dear I'm really going
to miss learning about
Pythagoras and Calculus
Horatio and Fortinbras
Philip Larkin and the Schlieffen Plan
because I love it so much
and I'm extremely concerned
about my impending examinations
and my future career in banking'

instead of
'Ya dancer!
am gonni spend aw day
lyin in ma pit lookin ut
hardcore porn on ma phone
an takin selfies uv ma tadger
an sendin it ti some wee lassie
coz am a lazy bastard
an so ur aw ma pals!'
or
'Ya dancer!
am gonni spend aw day
lyin in ma pit lookin ut
hardcore porn on ma phone
an takin selfies uv ma fanny
an sendin it ti some wee nyaff
coz am a lazy bastard
an so ur aw ma pals!'

yes
yes
I'm sure they will

in Boots the chemist
they've stuck
a zig-zaggy bumble-bee-coloured
length of tape on the floor
which you are forbidden
to cross

something like
a crime scene

you have to shout
what you're there for
and what you want until
everyone in
the immediate vicinity
knows you are
in desperate need
of *Viagra* or *Vagisil*
or *Vicks Vaporub*

anything
beginning with V

then you have
to lean at a disturbing angle
to pick up your bag of drugs
and shout your address
so everyone knows
where you live
and where to go
if there's a nationwide vacuum
of haemorrhoid cream

on the Breaking News channel
with the up-to-date death league
a gigantic in-your-face
green-haired Skype expert
with a variety of enticing chemicals
on the shelves behind her
is telling us the best way
to breathe in
and out
to reduce anxiety
and stress levels
when you're hopelessly
trying to find some *Andrex*

walking in the park
keeping six feet away
from all of humanity

wondering why
we're being asked
to accept
a projected
20,000 British dead
out of a population
of 68 million
as a major triumph
a big thumbs-up
a sigh of relief
while China has
only 3,200 deaths
out of a population
of one and a half billion

a scratch of the head
maths was never
my strong point

two children throw bread
at four swans

one helicopter hovers
in the far-off sky

someone's having a laugh

something else
is going on

social distancing
super-spreader
self-isolation
patient zero
ICU
PPE
total lockdown
elbow bump

R number
herd immunity
new normality
test and track
track and trace
trace and test

blended learning
excess deaths

I keep scrolling back
to add some more

happening acronyms
and phrases
sure to be included
in the first written history
of the coronavirus pandemic

if there's anyone
left to read it

two days ago they started
ripping up the road
with claw-machines

red plastic barriers
temporary lights

maintaining the power
upgrading the gas

or possibly
mass pits
for brisk disposal

the BBC are showing
repeats of *Miranda*
to keep the nation's
morale erect

instil the spirit of The Blitz
in delicate millennials
Generation Z

I hope there's
not a shortage
of razor blades in Tesco

we’re refining the details
of our little savings
and what to do if we’re
killed by the virus

make it easier
for those left behind

collate the mess

testaments
funeral music
power of attorney

objects of importance
value
sentimentality
a few sentences
about things we did

that’ll be fine
reasonably adequate

bank cards to cut-up
direct debits to be erased
as if we never

as a BBC correspondent
witters on in
a deserted Leicester Square
except for someone
on a bench with
a surgical mask
next to a statue
of Paddington Bear

a man walks up
behind her wearing
a tricorn hat
and an equally pointless
17th Century plague doctor's mask
with a protruding beak
to protect him
from miasmic air

stops
and looks around
then wanders off
looking for another patient
or a jar of marmalade

get the soap and get
a creamy erotic lather going
and sing
the Jacob Rees-Mogg version
of ‘Happy Birthday’ twice
or the Sex Pistols version
of ‘God Save the Queen’ once
and get that squidgy goodness
in between the fingers
and around the thumbs
and around the bit
where your hand meets your wrist
and the tips of the fingers
and up your nose
and into your ears
and right up your crack
until you’re completely knackered
and have to go for a wee nap

people are forbidden
to go to the pub
so they're buying lager
and congregating on
the closest
green space

a park
a pitch
a patch
of waste land

soft March sky
Mother's Day sun

an empty bevvy
is more important
than imminent death

today's noise
is more relevant
than tomorrow's silence

there’s a power cut
during the night

we only know because
a phone alarm went off
at ten past two

it’s gone
for an hour

black streets
integral services

we can hear them
trying to fix it
with drills and shouts

we create
two cups of tea

the façade of society
is already starting
to decay and fall

I slip stealthily
down
to the bins
being careful not to be seen
by the deviant-sniffing drones
armed with laser bazookas
or roving police patrols
who'll lay into me
with tasers
and truncheons
and screaming
'STAY AT HOME!
Putting bags of human waste
into your human grey bin
is not essential travel
you selfish essential BASTARD!'

standing at the glass
staring out at the cricket field

the oval of grass is empty
except for a man and his brown dog

I can see this man's arm
moving through air
as he hurls a ball as far as he can
with one of those ball-hurling contraptions

an elegant trajectory

the dog races and chases the ball
clamps it in its teeth and brings it back

untroubled
repetition
repetition

I can see this man's arm
moving through air
as he hurls a ball as far as he can
with one of those ball-hurling contraptions

an arc in space

the dog races and chases the ball
clamps it in its teeth and brings it back

standing at the glass
staring out at the cricket field

what are all the people I know
doing
right
now?

getting out of bed
eating a cereal
reading a book
watching a coronavirus update
conceiving a child
washing the dishes
writing a poem
writing a novel
eating a biscuit
committing murder
picking their nose
taking a dump
having a game of KerPlunk
starting a jigsaw
watching a box set of *George and Mildred*
watching a box set of *Breaking Bad*
watching a box set of *The Prisoner*
burying a body in the back garden
tossing a coin
having a cup of tea
listening to a siren
finishing a jigsaw
falling off a bike
watching a coronavirus update
contemplating the idiocy of humans
washing their hands
washing their clothes
going to bed
wondering what to do with
the rest of their lives
wondering what all the people they know
are doing
right now

I have an ear anomaly
affecting my balance
when I first get up

it’s not a spin
more of a tilt

a sideways plummet
as if the planet
has liberated itself
from its vertical axis
and is careering
through skins of time

the walls become
the ceiling and
the ceiling becomes
the walls

fair enough

I imagine it’s like
a benign high

peculiar but nice
to feel that nothing
is ever the same again

hair salons
have been ordered
to close immediately
along with bookmakers
and pubic waxers

a septuagenarian trim
is not considered essential
to the continuance of life
unlike tins of prunes
and mushy peas

bottom rolls
scented soap

there will be some
reckless experiments
carried out over
the next few months
with clippers and colourant

families emerging
squinting into the light
of a brave new world
with catastrophic hairstyles
and sutured scalps

bearded ladies
baldy children

cartoon-like tufts
exploding out at
extravagant angles
and irreparable damage
done to the national soul

concept arbers
78

Prince Charles has
tested positive

he was given the test
with a swab that has
a small crown
embossed on the cotton
and is now relaxing
with his gold-trimmed mask

maybe he'll take his chance
and sneak into
the Queens's bedroom
and cough in her ear
as she sleeps
then sneak out again

whispering
'Die Mommy Dearest, Die!'

I've washed my hair
every day since 1974
but now I'm not
bothering my arse

I've decided to let
my standards slip

they won't protect me
from Covid-19

I'll just avoid
looking in the mirror
and save a fortune
on *Head and Shoulders*

back in the flat
I can look out and see

our meandering trails
of footprints
on the wet grass
of the cricket field

the route we took
past silent gardens
swings and trampolines

a barbecue kit
basketball hoop

wooden sheds and wind chimes
a small face
at a kitchen window

a smaller face
at a bedroom window

two sets side by side
connecting then
diverging

preserved forever
in memory
like a dinosaur couple
newly extinct

claps and howls
and pots and pans
being defiantly banged

at eight in the evening
for the NHS

little silhouettes
in doorways
and windows

a distant
firework

a plane
continuing
to land

an orchestra of lost souls
a dissonant symphony
of hope and fear

because the Government
is incapable
of providing ventilators
unlike every other country
in the grown-up world
we've decided to
manufacture our own
using
sticky-backed plastic
and knicker elastic
and a vacuum cleaner hose
being shoved into
one of our mouths
while the other mouth
takes a deep breath
and blows down it
at regular intervals
for several months

in the middle
of the night
I’m too near the edge of the bed
and whack the lamp
with my arm
as I turn

my arm has
a mind of its own

Helen says ‘Jesus Christ!
What the hell was that?’
or words to that effect

I tell her

I tell her
to go back to sleep
which she does

half an hour later
I’m lying in the dark
thinking about death

the proximity
of non-existence

my mind has
a mind of its own

if Helen dies
I'll wait for a while
then disappear
and no one
will find me
for a long time
or possibly never

this is a unique moment
in history we're living through!
there has never been
anything like this before!
a televised global plague!
we should feel privileged!

what do you say
to that?

I say

you can shove
your privilege up
your arse

end of the month
I usually go to see
mum and dad's plaque
in the cloister
at Woodside

take their images
out of my wallet
and slide them in
at the edge of the words

talk to thin air
put down flowers
put the photos
back in my wallet

catch the bus

but I can't do it
anymore
because
it isn't essential
so I put the flowers
in a vase at home
prop the pictures
against the glass

the cabinet in
our room for living

one of mum
alone and smiling
mum and dad
on their wedding day

I'll let them stay
until the flowers die

I’ve thought of
a great wee lyric
about coronavirus
to be sung to the tune
of the middle bit
of ‘Ghost Town’
by The Specials

“Do you remember the good old days before coroni?
We wiped our bums and ate baked beans and macaroni”

it even rhymes

it’s something
to do with my time

2020 could be a record year
for the ingestion of books

I've just finished
The Drought by JG Ballard
followed by *The Amateur Emigrant*
by Robert Louis Stevenson
followed by *Goodbye to Berlin*
by Christopher Isherwood
and now I'm reading
That Was a Shiver
by James Kelman

in one story he mentions
charity shops where you
can buy pre-owned books
which made me quickly remember
from the numbness of my head
that I once bought a pre-owned copy
of *A Disaffection*
by James Kelman
in a charity shop in Tenby

what were the chances of that?
Tenby of all places!

I'll bet eight out of ten people
couldn't tell you that Tenby
is a seaside town in Wales
I'll bet you they couldn't
I'll bet you they couldn't

I keep a list

after *That Was a Shiver*
by James Kelman
I'll read *The Complete Stories*
by Franz Kafka

a single old lady
on the far side of the field

dark winter coat
anticlockwise

slowly past
the decrepit scoreboard

head bowed
to the wind

I feel like Rick Grimes
from *The Walking Dead*
every time I dash
to the shops to get
some free range eggs

watching out for walkers
shambling and drooling
up the middle of the road
or the infected pavement

next time I'll take
a metal spike with me
and run up and stick it
in the bad brain of anyone
who looks as though
they're about to enter
my two metre exclusion zone

maybe even some wee granny
who slightly glances
in my direction

TAKE THAT GRANDMA!

justifiable violence
for the equilibrium of society

could that be a niggly tickle
at the foot of my throat?

is that a snotty sniffle I've acquired
which isn't a symptom anyway
(or so the Tory doctors say)?

can I detect a fatal frontal ache in the head
caused by the onset of Covid-19?

or could it just be down to the fact
that I drank half a gallon of gin
last night

we'll never
know for sure

we've decided to hold
our very own
demonstration of appreciation
for the NHS
which consists of
standing at the window
shouting WE LOVE YOU NHS!
and clanging lids
and blowing bugles
and smashing bottles
and firing cannons
and detonating
sticks of Tesco dynamite
at midnight
when everyone has
finally fallen asleep
after yet another day
of self-isolating stupor
and they'll wake up
and think to themselves
'Hey, that's great!
We really hope you'll do it again!'

in the local store to get a bottle
of Helen's watermelon water
the only place
that has it
standing obediently
behind the strip of tape
on the floor waiting my turn
the man ahead
at the counter
buying urgent cigarettes
instead
of continuing
to the right and out the exit
decides to come back
the exact way he came
which will involve
skiffing right past me
at a distance of one foot
close enough to swallow
his particles
of breath
I quickly
step to my left
putting a required social gulf
between us
he moves past
without looking as if
I wasn't here I'm a ghost

you start to recognise
the individual arias
of birds outside
in the sunnyshine

achieve familiarity
with the patterns
of notes
rise and fall

particularly a blackbird
I've heard with
its orange beak

three notes repeated three times
in quick succession
a jaunty wee number
he must have picked up
from somewhere
a human whistle
a transistor radio

a pop hit from the 1970s

he's out there now
on a branch in the trees
tweeting for love

I can see him
without opening my eyes

three notes repeated three times
in quick succession

two bruiser polis
with yellow chests
and ominous helmets

zapping past
Paisley Abbey
on Apache attack bicycles

night-goggling the bus shelters
for illegal gatherings
of more than none

only the food bit
of M and S is still operating

through the door
you have to walk
an empty avenue
between the spectrum-coloured
quarantined Spring collections

cordoned-off mannequins
wearing man-made skirts
and sweatshop shirts

strangely touching
expressionless eyes
like something from
a hieroglyph

sacred systems
no longer used
convex mirrors
installed on the walls

wait for my slot
on the symbolised spot

go and buy
my vital chips

hmmm
I don’t exactly fancy the idea
of ending up in
a makeshift hospital
in some soulless conference centre
attached to ventilators
and Christ knows what else
with things beeping
and dripping and rumbling
and wires
tangling and snaking
until you wake one morning
to find yourself on the list
of the least likely to survive
the unwashed expendable
left to their own devices
and sealed up pronto
in special lead-lined caskets
or eco-friendly baskets
like something out
of Chernobyl
and burnt as fast
as you can with no one there
to wave byebye
but it might just come to that
it might just

we got on the train
and now we're hurtling down
the wrong rails
to Disasterville
via Fiasco Central
and Claptrap Junction

instead of
dodgy science
and heartbreaking tragedy
we could have had
controlled vision
and mature strategy

but it's too late
to leap off
no one with power
is going to confess
that we could have
travelled a wiser track

the moon at
the ending of March

a waxing crescent
in the sky to the west

jewel-like Venus
directly above

bewitching
mysterious
poetically inspiring

the stars don’t give
a flying fuck

our neighbour two floors below
likes putting plastic plants in pots
and turning the flat complex
into something resembling
a care home for
the mentally gubbed

I've concluded the only
reasonable course of action
is to report him to
the discreet 'Dob in a Dobber'
Paisley Gestapo viral dobline
and watch him being carted away
in a self-isolating strait-jacket
for crimes against insanity
and horticultural refinement

in Morrisons at Lonend
a wee lassie a wee lassie
is using a pointing pole
a directional prompt
to show me show me
exactly exactly
where to stand
two metres
making me
feel conspicuously thick
as a plank a plank
as I wait for a person
in front of me at the check-out
to finish filling their bags
of delight until it’s
my turn my turn

an article in the tabloid
says a dj set up
speakers and turntables
and dance lights
in his garden
and blasted out
rave classics all night
and everyone
in the street loved it
and he wants to do it again

just don't try it
round here bub

Donald Trump the cretinous cunt
has just told his fellow Americans
to hunker down
for a rough two weeks

and when those two weeks are up
he'll tell them it's going to be
another rough two weeks
possibly until
the end of time

at the end of which
he'll conveniently forget
he originally called it a Chinese hoax
and America would definitely
be open for business
by Easter no problemo!

then he'll boast
he warned about the virus all along
and it was his divine essence that beat it
and despite evidence on film
his pinhead followers will call him a hero
and volunteer in droves to carve his
orange liar face on Mount Rushmore

a child's rainbow
stuck in a window

is all we have

to protect us from
a serial-sniffing
projectile snotterer
riddled with bat dribble
from a grotty market
that flogs live cats
for dumb-clucks to eat

propped on his trolley

far too close
not giving a shit

we're working our way through box sets
of subsequent seasons of *The Twilight Zone*
as we have our tea
on trays on our laps

episodes about
astronauts thinking
they've landed on an asteroid
but it's Earth all the time

people escaping in a spaceship
to a distant planet to start a better life
which turns out to be Earth all the time

a man who's scared to fall asleep
as he knows he won't wake up again

it's better than watching
the Government's daily briefing

a lot more answers
a lot more believable

a man in a desert
withering with loneliness
a hitch hiker who turns out to be death

Helen's decided
in the absence of
a viable test for coronavirus
she's going to test me instead
for complete Baloneyvirus
which consists of sticking
the two first fingers
from both of her hands
right up my two nostrils
and going
ram-ram-ram
really hard up to my brain
and if I bleed to death
I haven't got it

waking and wondering
if this is the day I'll get
the persistent cough
and fever followed by
illumination isolation
hospitalisation ventilation
deterioration deathification
fossilisation speedycremation
a swift acceleration then getting
up and putting the toaster on

Helen shows me
my old pal Tommy Cherry's
latest coronaislanddisc
he's posted on Facebook

songs to help us
through the days

there's a picture
of the Stiff Records label
with the words
'New Rose' and The Damned

and Tommy
telling the story
of me telling him
that I have to pop in
to *Listen* record shop
at the top of Paisley High Street
and get this new single
and how a strange door opened
and life is never the same

44 years ago
a billion revolutions
per minute ago

I guess these things
have got to be

dreams are always first person
you never see yourself
it's always in
your own eyes

I'm forced into
the back of a truck
on Paisley High Street
we are going to be taken to
a concentration camp

crack-smoking poet
Craig Charles is
already in the truck
but I don't really speak to him
tell him to budge up

it's taking too long
so I jump out and
run all the way home
some men in a jeep arrive
as they're looking
for a way into the flats
I turn their
own machine gun on them
but it doesn't work so
I throw a grenade instead
which blows three of them up
until they're dead
the dream stops when I shout
'That was some sabotage!'

no doubt it's all
connected to anxiety
concerning coronavirus
dehumanisation
and personal invasion

or just a load of old bollocks

it’s beginning to rain

working out
tomorrow’s shopping list

yoghurt ✓
coffee ✓
tinfoil ✓

only 708 dead
in Britain today

prunes ✓
mustard ✓
low cal tonic ✓

it’s stopped raining

scampi ✓
chicken ✓
cranberry sauce ✓

things are looking up

in the eye of isolation
I've started yet another book
which is *M Train* by Patti Smith
and she mentions Jack Kerouac
early on which made me think
of his book *On the Road* which
is the only book in my life
I stopped reading halfway through
and chucked in the bin even though
I love the Beat poets
there was something
about the main characters
and their viewpoint which made me puke
offended me in some way I can't
really remember I hoped at first
he was being ironic he wasn't but
I like Patti Smith I'll finish this

a young phantom a trainee reaper
of indeterminate sex
gliding up Greenlaw Drive
with a white mask
a dark bag over its shoulder
and a Gregory Corso faustus hood
like something out of
a Max Von Sydow movie
in search of fresh souls
or a tin of chopped tomatoes

I was going to call
this sequence
Lockdown
but I've just found out
that Poet Laureate
Simon Armitage
has written a poem
also called
Lockdown
which is a real pain
so I open the blinds
and look out
and say 'Coronaworld'
as I inspect the unsound streets
which suddenly strikes me
as a much better title anyway
so ya boo sucks to Simon

I clean the row of old drinking mugs
on the shelf above
the kitchen door

I don’t do this very much

a coffee break graveyard
mugs with chips on the rim
handles missing
fault line fractures

weeks or more of oose
and dust

James Dean Gallery Fairmount Indiana
Tolpuddle Martyrs Museum
Chicago Untouchables Tour
Last Monday at Rio Poetry Night
Albert Einstein’s hair
Bonnie Prince Charlie
Discovery Point Dundee
Jessie Retirement Congratulations!

flawed remembrance
of fragments of time
I haven’t the strength
to chuck in the bin

the mug from Liberty Island
broken aesthetically in half
and glued back together

a thread-thin crack
straight through the crown
then cutting the NEW and
YORK in two

morning again
open the blinds
no one there

no cars no vans

a humdrum
Armageddon

the wee cat from
the house next to our flats
sitting on its back step
in the freezing light

we call her Nellie
she doesn't care
about global pandemics
economic tsunami
plateaus and symptoms

she likes chicken

she looks up
and sees me looking

no pollution no normal

a stabilising breeze
of apprehension

we see the same dogs
on the grass every day

two small white ones
we call belter and snuffler
two huge white ones
we call lollop and dollop

we don’t want to know
their real names

the spell will
be broken

a mad black pup
with a yellow hoop
who never knows
when to give up

going as fast he can then
even faster

helter and skelter
mutter and nutter

I’ve to check proofs
for a book of poems
being published in 2020

Chips, Paracetamol and Wine
prophetic title

typos

spacing
a click to the left
a click

to the right

but it’s not easy
to get it going
what’s the point
it doesn’t
feel that
important

or maybe it feels
too important

irrelevant meanings
in the relevant place

full stops

tonight we're watching
the Herzog version
of *Nosferatu*
with manifestations
of stupidity and plague

a scene near the end
with red wine drinkers sitting
at a long wooden table
in the cobbled square
surrounded by coffins
stuntrats
ratextras
and dancers

makes me
think of
the photos in today's papers
of crowds in London parks
doing sad stretching exercises
hot sunbathing
not caring about
comprehending
oblivious of
the concept of death
the finish of everyone

on a nerve-shredding expedition
into town trying not to catch it
I go into a Silk Street post office
to send a poetic parcel
completely essential
to a couple of friends

as I come up to the window
I can hear noises from something
the postmaster is watching
on an unseen screen
which sounds like a woman
having a startling orgasm
over and over louder and louder
accompanied by
ascending climactic music

it's either
a Marvel Comics superhero blockbuster
he's watching for escapist relief
from the misery all around us
or I've just interrupted him
having a non-essential wank

I think I'll get a tin of paint
and go around
the houses in my street
and paint a red cross
and a big
C
right below it
which stands for
corona or corpse
or contamination
on each of the doors
like something from
a less-enlightened age
in the confident belief
that everyone here will
kill themselves laughing
at the post-industrial irony
and won't even contemplate
smashing my bloody face in

down to the shop
to get some milk
back in ten minutes

easy peasy
in and out

is it now?
itinerant liquids
waiting in the air

the big once-a-week spree

probing as fast as I can
through Paisley Cross
past the cenotaph
and the boarded-up shops
like a Gulf War cruise missile
processing the precinct ahead
for potential hazards
knobheads and bozos

berks on bikes
Dawn of the Dead

infernal sneezers
wheezy coughers
in groups of three or four
who obviously aren't here
for any intrinsic reason

mucus misfits
men ejecting phlegm
women with Medusan hair

a forlorn queue
for a chemist or bank
hands in pockets
cash or
a drug

it's just what
we've always done
an imbedded instinct
to rhythmically return
to somewhere that once
used to mean something

the something long dissolved

someone soaping their precious car
someone mowing their front lawn
someone pumping some air
into a tyre

someone trying to make someone breathe
someone alone in a sterile cell
someone unable to hold
a hand

at the entrance to Tesco
I scoosh a square of cloth
with fluid
from a plastic bottle
and wipe the handle
of my medium-deep trolley
to keep death at bay
for a little bit longer

I stock up
on onions
and lemons

I don't have a glove
so I prod the pin number keypad
with my finger sheathed
in a piece of kitchen towel
I smuggled into the shop
when no one was looking

preparation is everything
in the act of creation
or destruction
pleasure or pain

maybe I should check ebay
to see if they have
a Kevlar-coated catsuit
or a silver tinfoil cast-off
from *The Andromeda Strain*?

here's praying
cuddly Boris Johnson
who's triggered
a nifty immortality move
by catching Covid-19
and is now beyond criticism
recovers soon

so he can
be canonised
as fast as possible
and hurry back to being
the exemplary lying racist
blundering philandering sexist
self-submerged arrogant egoprick
that we all know and loathe

pressing TEXT
on the telly
to get some of
the old fashioned
heart-warming stories
of empathic togetherness
that don't make it onto
the breaking news

a man coughing
on a policeman
and saying he has Covid-19

right

scammers going into
pensioners' houses
saying they're from
Health and Safety
and robbing them blind

okay

two men walking
into Sainsbury's
and licking their fingers
then smearing it over the meat
and vegetables
and door handles

that's it

click on the kettle
tune in to the comforting
daily-death-totals instead

I like waking and remembering
that today there is nothing to do
nowhere to go

that magic feeling

the insistence of having
to do things and go somewhere
to authenticate my existence
has been erased

there’s no mail to look at
as there’s no mail

there’s no sun to look at
as there’s no sun

there’s nothing to stop me
doing nothing

I’ll go and write a poem anyway
simply because I don’t have to

I'm beginning to wonder
if unfettered lengthening
of unsightly nasal hair
is one of the symptoms
of coronavirus

I've never done
as much plucking in my life

every time I look
there's another
long white hair
straggling down
from one of
my nostrils
usually the left

fever
cough
nose-pube

it makes no sense
it all makes sense

a cluster of
empty silver-green ampoules
on the ground beneath
the wooden bench
at the edge of the field

no doubt
isolators come here
to ingest a chemical
that helps them cope
with social distancing

takes their minds off
the catastrophic effect
that coronavirus
is having on
the economy

assists them
to come to terms
with the huge death toll
of over 40,000 people
that has just been announced

or maybe
they just like
the thrill of things
going into their brains
and bursting out of their skulls

someone has pushed over
the large black waste bin
outside the church
on Greenlaw Drive

of course

it's on the Government list
of tolerated activities

going for shopping
going for medicine
exercising the body
pushing over a waste bin

I must remember
next time I pass
a plebeian bin

church-going
isn't permitted

I'm baptising all the basics
with an antiseptic wipe

plastic bag of oven chips
plastic container of milk
plastic tubes of flavoursome water
wrappers for *Twirl* and *Dairy Milk*
which may or may not be plastic

some other satanic substance
Frankensteined by man

we used to watch
the media briefing
with three people standing
two metres apart
at lecterns with Union flags
behind them

journalists on long screens
asking the same questions
about lack of testing
deficient protection
day after day

politicians
robotically mouthing
the same non-answers
to entirely different questions

now we turn it down
and do something
useful instead

change the channel
talk to each other

break wind
break news

the weeks go by

thank you good night
STAY AT HOME
SAVE LIVES
SPEAK SHITE

in my clapped-out brain
I'm the Last Man on Earth
lone plodder of the end-time
reverently following
familiar worn routes
of the dead streets of Glasgow
magnificent desolation
no jugglers and buskers
fire-eaters and unicyclists
evangelists and partisans
passing black entrances
buzzers
doors
that used to be
taken for granted like people
love sympathy inspiration
they'd always be there
now they're not
just like that
bookshops
bus stops
cinemas
stations
halls
studios
printers
galleries
museums
Koolba Indian restaurant
please God
anything but the Koolba

from the window
I can see our local 20 bus
which we call The Diddler
bang on time
five past nine

the punctuality
has been extraordinary
over the past three weeks
thanks to the fact
it's not picking anyone up
or dropping
anyone off

no passengers is best
passengers are a pest

that's the key
to tick-box efficiency
they'll have to remember
when the auld lang synes return

listen to this
it sounds like
there's a small dog
trapped inside
the tumble dryer
going round and
round yes a small dog
is trapped in
the burning
spinning metal
machinery making
a desolate yelp
at circular intervals
it goes round
and round with the rest
of the things the socks
underpants
towels and more
underpants I imagine
what sort of dog it is
a small white dog
with pure black eyes
making this agonised
yelp as if it's begging
for help a petrified yelp

Easter Sunday
resurrection

the paper is put through
the letterbox
by our valiant boy
in his anti-crematorium suit

coffee and toast
917 dead yesterday
Britain set to have
the highest death toll in Europe
because of smug ineptitude
criminal bungling

procrastination
masturbation

we'll only know
things are getting back to normal
when the *Sunday Mail* headline
is about an honest gangster
called 'The Hamster'
or 'The Pangolin' who's
just been gunned down
in an Asda toilet

we must all pray
for this day to come soon

thank God for
small something or
others

we've got it easy
we wake up
swallow coffee
turn the pages of papers

do the puzzles
read about
the existential silliness
of football

the necessity
of the dreams
in our days

we don't have
to race out to work
we don't have parents
we don't have
to teach our children
at home
about theorems
and trigonometry
the correct moment
to put an apostrophe

the lost art

of Scottish precipitation
vivisection
atom splitting
for beginners

we can look out
at the weather
as its actually happening

as its doing what

it is made to do

(I think I missed
an apostrophe or two

I was never much good
at the placement
of punctuatio)n

we watch *Death in Venice*
which features an epidemic
everyone wants to ignore

it slunk from the east
a human feast

Venice awash
with generous sloshes
of milky disinfectant

beautiful stinky canals
burning piles of elegant rubbish

the body count
beginning to mount
a black tear
running down the side
of Dirk Bogarde's corpse-face

art drained
of soul or heart

out of control disease
is bad for business
it will totally bugger-up
the economy

bury it under
the time-worn carpet

Tadzio's slinky bum
silhouetted against the sun
as he turns into a Greek statue

a malevolent minstrel
sticking out his tongue

the faces of the dead
are starting to appear
on the television screen

smiling men and women
in digital lines
here then not

no longer just
graph-curves
national totals
revised on a daily basis
as the thousands pile upon
thousands

a woman is telling us
about her dad who has
just had his ventilator removed
as there's no more
that can be done

she said some words to him
on the telephone

her mother
waits alone

the nurses
at his side
easing him into nowhere

that's all

the NHS is crying out
for more vital testing
to be done so they can
get doctors and nurses
back into the hospitals

meanwhile
Iagoesque creep-toad Michael Gove
pulls some strings
and gets a test carried out
on his un-vital daughter
then goes out jogging
in breach of self-isolation rules
and tries to deny
he is breaking any rules
then twists it
when he knows the game is up

one law for him
another for scum

thank you Govidiot for being
a consummate stereotype

repugnance needs to be
topped up from time to time

I've noticed some
of the recent poems
have included less lyrical content
and introduced more
politically-charged content
a sharp tone of
simmering belligerence

this is because
as the days roll by
it's becoming increasingly apparent
the Conservative rulers have
awe-inspiringly mismanaged
and miscalculated
the whole tragedy
resulting in
many more avoidable deaths
and family suffering
and are now content
to wait it out
until they can finally
take the credit when it's over
and deny anything was wrong
and lead a collective sing song
of 'We'll Meet Again'
in Westminster Abbey

I'm hunting for
Cardamom Pods in Morrisons
and can hear a woman
in the aisle next to me
coughing her guts up
a bit like this ...

she should
be in bed
or an ICU
(*I See You*)

I give her a berth
as wide as the Clyde

I can hear her again
an aisle behind
as I scrabble about
for zero fat yoghurt

creamy
and Greek

as I prepare to enter
the gauntlet of death
with the green spots
telling you where to stand
as you queue for the tills
she steers in front of me
coughing her guts up
a bit like this ...

which makes me reverse
at the speed of light
and reminds me to go
and get some prunes

we're okay sitting here
in a sort of security
ethereal cocoon

sleep
do things
sleep

secure in the knowledge
we don't know what
will happen next

we do know
the old and frail
are allowed to die
in care home hell
like something
from a history book about
some unbelievable century
full of wickedness
and horror

dying in their chairs
and beds
untreated and terrified

lost inside
themselves

not even given the dignity
of being included
in the latest statistics

things are bad when
I have to keep on
looking in the thesaurus
or on the internet
for alternative words
that mean the same
as terrified

synonyms
that will give some variety
subtle inflections
expressive slants

some are okay
like afeared
or frightened
or shit scared

but none are as good
as terrified

I'll stick
with that

terrified
terrified
terrified

enough of coronavirus
for one day

it's Julie Christie's 80th birthday
so we're going to watch *Demon Seed*
about a woman impregnated
by a randy computer
which carries the sum
of human knowledge

synthesised semen
needles and probes
unloving insertion

somehow it
seems applicable

ignorance and wisdom
the rape of the planet
the brokenness of Man
for each of us to see

fun-packed Government-
endorsed instructions
are available
showing us how to
make our own
Covidbuster facemasks
using
string
elastic
the sleeve of a shirt
a piece of fabric
covered in the pattern
of the Overlook Hotel carpet
in *The Shining*

or a dissected bra
with plunge or full cup
being utilised
to accommodate
the shape of the available face

if that isn't convenient
then a pair of
soiled underpants
will suffice

a big sweaty
Rab C. Nesbitt simmet
with lots of holes

Here's Johnny!

just breathe normally

on the field we find
a dirty twenty pence piece

which had been stomped
into the grass
long ago
and has now returned
to the surface

like the bones
sometimes do
on old battlefields

self-exhumation

evidence of
the previous life

bent in the centre
a bright scar
through the head
of the Queen

the year obscured
or maybe never there
to begin with

minted in nowhere
worthless to everyone
except us

we'll put it on
our mantelpiece
for luck

next to the pound
we'll find next week

because of coronavirus
March 2020 was the first March
in almost 20 years
that there hasn't been
a school bloodbath in the USA

a baby-faced wacko running amok
because he didn't get the best grades
or make it onto the basketball team

helicopter views of children
running with their hands up

the air is filled with the sweet sound
of twittering birds
instead of the sound
of a head being shot

disgruntled nutjobs
are sitting at home
self-isolating
with posters
of the Columbine killers
stuck to their bedroom walls

cleaning their rifles
polishing their rocket launchers
and sending tweets
to the state senator
demanding a compensatory
financial package is put in place
and their human right
to slaughter swotty students
is respected

old Captain Tom has raised 17 million
for the NHS so far by doing 100 laps
of his garden with his walker

a wee granny in Sutherland
is now raising dosh by climbing
a mountain on the stairs in her home

I've decided I'm going to raise money
by carrying out a sponsored assassination
of rubbish cabinet politicians

or more realistically by eating a bacon
and brown sauce bap each day for the rest
of my life or until I have a heart attack

it's a lovely day
tomorrow

standing in
the butcher's queue
feeling like Arthur Askey
or Gracie Fields
clutching the coupons
for my weekly ration
of scrag end
intestines
waiting meekly
for a V2 rocket
to land on my head

run rabbit
run rabbit
run
run
run

tomorrow is
a lovely day

behind me
a man removes
his mask
sneezes
puts it back on

there should be almost
nothing on the street

an intrepid hunter/gatherer or two
heading for the weekly shop
in their car
there and back
quick as a flash

steadfast consumers
conscientious dependents

instead
trying to cross Glasgow Road
is like trying to avoid
getting killed at Piccadildo Circus
trying to cross the road
in Calcutta or Saigon
Rome or Amman

the Monaco Grand Prix
the Monte Carlo Rally
rolled into one

racing boys screeching along
as if screeching is going
out of fashion

lobotomy rhythms
lockdown my arse

just step off the kerb
and hope for the best
combined with a blind prayer

there's a perverse pleasure
to be derived from looking
at the bulging catalogue
of mistakes and misjudgements
the incompetent Government
has built up over the last few weeks
as they play lotto
with thousands of lives

ignoring warnings
fixation with Brexit
herd immunity theory
Johnson shaking hands
not answering questions
allowing mass gatherings
making people too scared
to go to GPs and A&E
no testing at airports
delaying lockdown
care homes
testing
equipment
protection

and speculating
on the next additions
premonitions

ignoring warnings again
ending lockdown too soon
delaying second lockdown
becoming increasingly defensive
denying that bad decisions were made
lack of morgues for second wave
botched vaccine production
botched vaccine distribution
care homes again
testing again
equipment again
protection again
letting Dominic Raab become PM

when Johnson shoots himself
letting Michael Gove become PM
when Raab shoots himself

I’ve heard that Denmark
is thinking of
opening up hairdressers
again

maybe I could
charter a plane
and get my dome done
in Copenhagen

or even just find
a wee rowing boat

take my chances
on the North Sea

it's TV time for the clod-
brain Americans again
who are out on the steps
with their AR-15s

for some reason they believe
the pandemic threatens
their right to bear arms
and shoot racoons

gun-toters
gunmakers

not quite able to grasp
the concept of
the virus
thinking
it's some conspiracy
conjured by a consortium
of socialist Bond villains
to blunt their rights
tell them what they can
or cannot buy in
the neighbourhood Walmart

burgers and fries
full metal jacket

TRUMP/PENCE
LIVE FREE OR DIE
GIVE ME LIBERTY
OR GIVE ME DEATH

the plague is here
death it shall be

some people make an effort
to give each of us
enough space
as they move
to the right or
the left with a
smile and a nod
depending on which
side of the road we're going
up or down

others you can see
from a mile
away
usually
wearing shades aren't
going to move in
the slightest because they have
it in their head that they're
some kind of revolutionary
free spirit when
in fact they're only
ludicrous fuckwanks

everything seems just to be
the way it will always be
getting the dinner ready
putting food in the oven
opening tins
selecting cutlery
sauce
taking food out of the fridge
putting food back in the fridge
looking out the window
at someone else walking
the pavement
leading a dog
everything seems
in the sun

out there

in the sun
people are dying in
their hundreds all the time
not far from here
theatres of horror
exhaustion pain
everything seems
replayed replayed
mortuary morgue
devotion care
death
alone
families unable to say
goodbye I love you
no end
it's like it's just going
to go on and
everything seems to be
replayed replayed
mortuary morgue
you have
to be sane
you have to be the same

the way it will always be
always

instead of
enduring Prime Minister's-
I-won't-give-a-straight-
*answer-to-a-single-*Questions
from the House of Commons
starring Dominic Raab
instead of
Boris Johnson
who's sitting at Chequers
chomping a tin of *Quality Street*
and watching streams
of *Love Island*
and *Sex in the City*

I'll go and do something
more uplifting
like watching
two little spiders
two feet apart
above the curtains
in the bedroom
who have hardly moved
in two days but
are definitely not dead
the first of which
we've called Bob Speedron
and the second of which
we've called Bruce Speedron
who are obviously
madly-spidery in love
but also wish to obey
the social distancing rule

at the start of lockdown
people were finger-
waggingly warned
not to come in
at all costs
not
to make a nuisance
of themselves

tumbleweed is now
rolling
in slow
motion
through empty
GP fortress-clinic
waiting rooms

Oops
maybe we went
too far!

folk are so scared
they'll stoically
embrace cancer
and heart disease
and strokes and
anything else they can
think of
instead of asking
for help

the country is dying
of unthought efficiency

an online isolation fitness class
for mothers and children
is infiltrated by
two men who
suddenly appear
on screen
having a Jodrell Bank

they must have
planned it for ages thinking
I say chaps
what's the best way
we can contribute
to the nation's ongoing battle
against coronavirus
and boost the flagging morale
of our beleaguered people?
I know!
Let's join in with
a group of young mothers
and their children
in leotards
and masturbate
in front of them
THEY'LL LOVE IT!

the selflessness and ingenuity
of the British spirit
knows no bounds

the sun's oot
I go to the garage
to get the table and chairs
so we can sit outside
without taking any exercise
except for opening a book
lifting a glass
forgetting about
the fucking virus

colours of death

I collide my head
on the jaggy corner
of the open flip-over door
blood starts
to ooze from
the flap-of-skin hole
I've created on my skull

an extra orifice

I don't think it's penetrated
all the way to the mainbrain
which is just as well
as I don't want to go
to the hospital and ask
for a transplant
as they'll tell me to sling
my hook
come back
after Christmas

cotton wool
and *Savlon* will do

horror-movie red
is smeared and clotted
in my hair
no one can have
experienced pain like this before

not even in child birth
I'm happy to be
just another gallant martyr
in the war against the plague

a hammered bampot
in the sun
with no shirt on
after an afternoon's
coronarefreshment
is kicking a football
up the road
singing
'Hello Hello
We are the Billy Boys!'

thus creating
what will
soon become
the deeply moving
community ritual
sing-a-sectarian-song
in support of the NHS
every Friday at 5 pm

Donald Trump has suggested
that everyone with Covid-19
should be injected
with disinfectant
or flooded inside
with ultra violet rays

clean the lungs
bring the light
into the body

why did no one else
think of this?
the man is a genius

I'm certainly going
to make sure
I'm first in line
when they start
the disinfectant injections
down at
Paisley Grammar School

or go and tan
a bottle of *Domestos*
pour myself
a Dom and tonic

Dettol on the rocks

cut out the middle man

feel the lovely
cleansing darkness
running through my veins

sitting under
the cherry blossoms

they'll fall soon
be gone

delicate archipelagos of cloud
light dazzling a flat-roof aerial

a girl's voice lifted on
the breeze saying
'pessimistic or
optimistic or
realistic'

the last sound
of coalescence

the human race
is clever and
stupid

'Jolene' coming
out of a window

ambulance music
on the Glasgow Road

two blackbirds
hopping about the field

picking up limbs of twig
splinters of stalks
in their beaks
for their nests

they go on
as we go
they don’t think
about us
what we want

we call them
Hopper and Dennis

they’ll inherit the Earth
don’t even know it

our death is with us
around us inside us

look it straight in the eye
if it has an eye

hold its hand
smack its gob

plant a kiss
rip the piss

don’t be afraid
to be bitter and twisted

here are some establishment
gold-medal winning poets

invited by their society
to post about Covid-19

elite syllable-twiddling
on a jaw-dropping scale

luvvies reaching to
out-profound each other

synonyms for insight
slapped on with a trowel

look-at-me-I'm-so-sensitive
fannying at the edges of death

(but I've always liked Ian McMillan
and his are pretty good I think)

there’s nowhere
I want to phone

no one I want
to Zoom with

or whatever
the latest latest is

chat words
buzz groups

the other way
around

the world is huge
the world is

everyone I need
is already here

in my local post office/
nicknack outlet to get
two powder-blue facemasks

six second class stamps please
and two of your finest
completely useless
comedy hospital facemasks
my good woman
and make it snappy

here are four of
your English guineas
as payment for these
delightfully life-enchanting
facial accessories
made in Taiwan
with any luck
as they know how
to handle a pandemic

and a packet of
Salt and Vinegar crisps

I'm ready now
to take on the air

inhale the future

HEROES
LEBARA
PLEASE QUEUE FOR SHOP HERE
1000 UK mins
1000 UK texts
100 international mins
lebara.co.uk
Trustpilot
FACE MASKS £2.00
SANITIZER HAND GEL INSIDE SHOP
Help everyone stay safe by social distancing
PLEASE QUEUE HERE FOR SHOP
PROTECT OUR #RETAIL HEROES

pink snow
on the grass

my scalp-gouge
is scabbing nicely

a crisp dark crescent
on my poor
Scottish flesh

blood moon
blossom sky

my brain
tried to escape
but failed
miserably

I'm here to stay

dreary clouds
the first for days

after the minute's silence
I buy a bunch of flowers
in Tesco

a friend has died
and I'm going
to lay them on
the front doorstep

leave a card
go back down the path

if Margaret is
at their window
I'll blow a kiss
press my hand to the glass
tell her we'll hug her
when this is
all over and
we're

back

to

normal.

I unpeel
the price sticker

a man walks past
and says
whit di yi call this then?

as he smiles at the sky

the start of the rain
eases my way

the occasional stillness
lowering of eyes

the Thursday clap
clatter of pans
in gratitude to
the working dead

recycled tears
shed
ready
to be used again

it's even now
exactly like
the yearly remembrance
of the First World War

lions led by donkeys

the cliché is true

Covid fodder
sold out by fools
who won't have to
account for themselves
when all of this is done

I went back through
the poems
because
I thought I was
possibly using
the word death too much

I wouldn't want it
to get tedious
for the reader

but the alternatives
are a bit keech

grim reaper's
a bit rural
termination's
a bit clinical
obliteration's
a bit apocalyptic

it is
what
it is

it is
death

I counted about 18 deaths
give or take 1 or 2
the proper tally is unknown

actually
it's probably not enough
so here are some more

death death death

death death death

the recommendation now
is that we wear facemasks
when we step on a bus
or stand in a shop

the rest of the Earth
has been doing it for weeks
saving souls
with effortless reason

our corpse inventory
makes them look like
top-ranking amateurs

the ‘guided by science’ mantra
is spewed out
and the Government insist
that the benefit of masks
is practically non-existent
but it probably won’t
do any harm

oh
go on then

they refuse to admit
that everywhere else
did it right
and we did it wrong

mask on for the first time
feeling like
a superhero
or a supervillain

Fatman
The Piddler

only two wandering mortals
in the whole of Tesco
are wearing one

nobody really
gives a toss

Green Wanker
Mad Shatter

I search down
the one way system
when I should be searching up

redirected breath
makes my glasses mist over
so I can't be sure
of what I hope I'm buying

Irn-Bru Man
Mister Cheese

without hope
we have nothing

I wish I could read
sign language for
the hard of hearing
because
I'm pretty sure
the sign language man
in a shiny suit
in the bottom
right hand corner
of the telly
during
the daily briefing
is actually saying things like
hawdon jist a wee minute
ah kin see whitz writtun
oan thur bits uv paper
an thur talkin
a complete loaduv pish
thur a dirty bunch
uv lyin arseholes

the shadowy advisors
are considering
asking people
to take their own temperatures
before they leave home
as if anyone is going
to do that
or maybe
there'll be
a shifty man in uniform
outside Paisley Gilmour Street
who'll order you to wheech down
your breeks and pants
and tell you to
spread your butt cheeks baby
so he can insert
his impressive
Boris-class heat-
seeking thermometer
into your passage
and then your mouth
because that's the way
we do it in Britain
and no Johnny Foreigner
from Germany or Korea
is going to show Us what to do

the follow-the-science scientists
are saying it's not fair
to compare Britain's
horrific death total
with the death totals
of other countries
e.g. Germany Italy Spain
as there are other factors
to be taken into consideration
and every nation
has individual characteristics

which must mean
there is something unique to Britain
that explains why we have
the worst death total in Europe
and the worst death total
per capita in the world
I wonder what
that intriguing quality is?
could it possibly be
our nauseatingly
incapable Government?

a girl with
a fur-lined parka hood

doing little gymnastics
on the fence that runs
alongside the steps

chucking stones
into the water
at the Hammills

a yellow bag
gently turning
in the bubble and plop

there’s no longer a honk
from the tannery
skinned animals
are not essential

but you can
smell lockdown
in the air

sense the current
of restless hunger

the green circles
on Morrisons floor

the flat planets
with the yellow arrows
saying *Please Queue Here*

are scuffed and scratched
and fading away
to a blackboard-duster
chalky white

the thousands of shoes
have taken their toll

rivers
of feet

oceans
of toes

in a few weeks
they'll be gone altogether
and we won't have a clue
what to do

as she passes the receipt
the check-out girl
suddenly quickly tells me
that she's washing
her hands so much
and squirting on sanitiser
and slapping on cream
and washing her
hands so much she can
feel her fingers all oily
and slippy when she taps
her pad she can feel them
slipping and can't get rid
of this feeling of slipping

Helen posted a response
to a Government-sponsored message
on Facebook which had said
how well it's all going and
how well the Government
have handled it
and how we must all continue
to flatten the curve

Helen's response said that
the NHS and the military
are wonderful
but that
the incompetent Government
and the way
they dealt with the crisis
have been woeful

somebody replied
said *Shut up!*

somebody replied
called her *Knobhead!*
with extreme prejudice

it was probably
Michael Gove

the massive temporary hospitals
are lying empty
no one to save

the single thing that was done well
is a waste of time
because the experts' projections
were pap
always flawed

but surely it's better
to be safe than sorry?

in that case
instead of a grand gesture
for public consumption
maybe they should have
been safe and sound
by creating reserves
of test-kits gowns
gloves masks and ventilators
months years ago
established a plan
for care homes
as we knew this would
happen
eventually

all the effort dedication
and sweat was misdirected
a fine achievement
symbolic elephant

coronavirus
has made it clear
to ourselves
what a self-
indulgent
spoilt
shallow
society we are
with our sad obsessions
money
media
cars
sex
sport
planes
haircuts
celebrity
takeaway coffee
instant gratification
excess of everything
lemmings heading
towards the precipice
and when
it's all over
we'll just go back
to the way we were
probably even more
and the damned planet
will be choked fucked

reading the book
Midnight in Chernobyl

which leads me to look
at photographs
of what Pripyat looks like now
on Google Images

trees rampant
where concrete once
was omnipotent

sterile Soviet architecture
a daft ferris wheel
far too human
a statue of an angel
blowing a trumpet

it can't be an angel
but that's what it looks like

a fox in the snow
swimming pool
sunglare through
the glasnost windows

in particular
a dodgem car arena
in an amusement park

mock headlights and steering wheels
a blanket of leaves
blown-in litter
rust and moss

some with spray-paint graffiti
by lads who have snuck inside
risking eternity

they were used
for only two hours

before the city was abandoned

fragile
bewilderingly beautiful
touchingly stupid

conductor rods
reaching to the roof of heaven
how the end could be

I'm frightened to peep
over the rim of
the communal
green food bin
which has just
been emptied
but I can't resist

it's a mini-Chernobyl
a minging meltdown

unhosed for months

unimagined new colours
unchristened fascinating lifeforms
sludging at the bottom
in the corners
and bends

Heinz Cream
of Bacteria Soup

monstrously entertaining
biological throbbings
multi-legged squirmings

don't stare for too long
in case they notice you
and take hold

consecrate your soul

a Council initiative
plastic reactor
fermenting the future

people are producing
a lot more natural waste
than usual

the next excreta

of evolution

it has to go somewhere

we go to
our friend David's funeral
in a cemetery north of Barrhead

there are more than
the authorized number of mourners
but everyone thinks what the hell
we're going to say farewell
whether they like it or not

death goes on regardless
of parliamentary decrees
panicky proclamations

people spaced well apart
except for the close family
who cling to each other
as real as can be

a mound of earth
beneath a tarpaulin

what a moment
it is to die

we drop roses
into the open grave

they fall out of sight
they're probably still
falling

there's a hint of sun
and sometimes rain

on the gravepath
two old biddies brush past us
insanely close

they must be following
the six inch rule
instead of
the six feet rule

we forgot to clap tonight
ring our bells
clang our lids

we looked at the clock
time had passed

it was 9 o'clock
and 8 o'clock
was no longer here

we were watching something
and showing our thanks
had slipped away
from our heads

like forgetting
a birthday card

remembering
who we thought we are

it's been a strange day
both of us beyond this street
for the first time in 8 weeks

we could do it now
but neighbours would think
we were mental
inform the police

standing at our glass
sending noises into the night
clapping when we shouldn't

we'll bang twice as hard
next week

Saul Bass would have been 100 today
if he hadn't died in 1996

he designed the titles for *Psycho*
and storyboarded the shower scene
persuaded Hitchcock to use a lot of
fast
cuts

we're going to watch *Psycho* as a tribute
if we can remain conscious

we keep on waking
at 5 in the morning

the birds
at dawn

I wonder if there's anyone else
self-isolating in the world tonight
who's going to have their very own
Saul Bass 100th birthday tribute

some native in the Amazon jungle
settling down with his DVD
and a piranha supper
wondering if there's anyone else out there
doing what he is

bog-standard madness
the insanity of survival

we discuss the possibility
of setting up
a Roger Corman/
Edgar Allan Poe-themed bus tour
which starts in Paisley
then heads
to Spain
for a night in Castle Medina
with optional pendulum torture
and harpsichord entertainment
then goes
to America
for a night in the House of Usher
with silent painting classes
provided by Roderick
followed by burial alive
for a modest supplement
and finishes
in an English banqueting hall
with bowls of hot gruel
and blind country dancing
led by Verden and Ligeia
and a farewell sing-along
of 'Molly Malone'
before heading back to Paisley

we don't
get out enough

later
on the way back from Tesco
I consider including
Prince Prospero's Bingo
cocktails called *Black Cat*
Cataleptic Karaoke
and a poster saying
COR! MAN! ALL OF THIS
AT A BARGAIN PRICE!

but that would be
a bit too much

it's Helen's 65th birthday
so I wrap her pressies
and do her cards
which I bought in WH Smith
from a harassed lad
behind a screen
who said he was
really worried about
a second wave of infections
after Boris Johnson's
Sunday speech

he can see it now
everyone rushing about
willy-nilly

I waved and told him
to keep on going
he's doing a great job

on the envelopes
I write things like
LOCKDOWN LOVE
and PANDEMIC PASSION
and SELF-ISOLATING SOPPINESS
and YOU'RE MY VERY OWN
SUPER-SPREADER
in an effort to make it
as special as possible

I would have written
HERD IMMUNITY HUMP
but it doesn't make sense
and I've run out of cards

a thorn
pricks the end
of Helen’s finger

as she places
her birthday flowers
in a vase

a gift
of blood
from a Covid rose

an oystercatcher
on the cricket pitch
with long orange legs
and long orange beak

jabbing for worms
next to
a white gull
and black crow

it shouldn't be here
it should be
at Loch Craignish
on the low tide mud
or chasing waves
at Craignish Point

it doesn't belong
in this viral town

I guess it was visiting
its magpie pals
and had to stay
when lockdown began

a woman jogger
puffs and pechs
up the steep path

a shaded incline
beside the abandoned zoo
that used to be
the abandoned bandstand

the purple apparatus
in the park
are out of bounds
with red and white tape

the playground
is also taped and forbidden
but a man is letting
his toddler play in it anyway

the look on his face says
just try and stop me

monkey bars
tyres on chains

the café
is shuttered

the grass
hasn't been cut
for weeks

it's carpeted
with daisies and buttercups
dandelion clocks

a coronavirus eco-system
to heal the planet

two young men
in a cloud of vape
on the verge beside
the miniature railway

locked-up
for the duration of
lockdown

one wearing
a Bill and Ben hat
one wearing
a baseball cap
with the word
EXPLORE on it

playing
'Shakin' All Over'
on a square black machine

on the municipal golf course
I swish my sodden shoes
through the long rough
looking for balls
like I did
when I was a kid

I find one which
is hollow and cracked
flooded with gunk

Noodle brand
not made in China

I also discover
a *Wagon Wheels* wrapper
and a red flag on a pole
lying at the fringe
of an island of trees

the cups on the greens
are full of brown water
which could be drunk
in the event
of an emergency

it feels strange
straying so far
I'm waiting for a loudspeaker
from nowhere
asking me what
I think I'm doing

I'm looking for golf balls
is what I will say
just before they take me away

I read that 80,000 people
died in Britain
during
the Hong Kong flu outbreak
in 1968 and 1969

80,000!
I hadn't a clue

I vaguely recall the name
but I don't remember
any change to the way we lived
no lockdown
facemasks
isolation
distancing
emotional mayhem
economic cataclysm

I don't remember
anyone fretting about it
wringing their hands
tearing their hair

we went on holiday
played in the street
hugged each other
went to the barber
did Christmas

everyone got on with it
and if you caught it and died
then that's the way
it crumbles
cookie-wise

ignorant blissheads
space age shruggers

now we swallow too much
demand too much

think we understand too much

a lot of small knowledge
is a dangerous thing

to remind us to clap tonight
I've stuck a sticky green sticker
to the tip of my nose
with the words CLAP AT 8 PM
written on it in biro

up until 8 we're watching
The A Word TV drama
which we recorded two days ago
and is about people
who don't fit the word *normal*

I can't see the words
but Helen can

I'm counting on the belief
that just knowing
I've got a sticky green sticker
stuck to my nose for some reason
will do the trick

as I pass a newspaper stand
I notice the headline
on *Weekend Sport*
which says
FREE SEX TOYS
FOR NURSES

next to a photo
of a happy young woman
with resplendent breasts

I just hope it isn't
the Government
who is ordering them

penis substitutes from Turkey
the wrong batteries from Iran

they'll be waiting a long time
for DIY ecstasy

someone made a quick film
of a young roe deer
with its cute horns
at the junction of
Buchanan Street
Bath Street
at six in the morning

nothing else awake
except a landing pigeon
and the worker who saw it
from the doorway
of Sainsbury's

it probably came
from the Necropolis
about three quarters
of a mile away
to see what's happening
with the human race

city of the dead
city of the living

it's listening
outside a Rolex shop
but it's not wearing a watch
and doesn't have any money
to buy one

it's a wonderful world
it isn't afraid

I wouldn't hang around
for too long little deer

run all the way
home to the gravestones

the two-legs
are coming back

I've nearly finished reading
Hello America
by JG Ballard

written
in 1981

which is concerned
with the future
45th President of the United States
who just happens to be
a criminal psychopath
with his finger itching
on the nuclear button

there's even talk
of a deadly virus

sounds
naggingly
familiar

I'm sure he'd love
to push that button
as a goodbye gesture of vengeance
when he finally has to leave
the last raspberry
of the man-child demon

a giant laser image
of Charles Manson
filling the sky

there's only a few pages to go
I'll let you know how it ends

in a selfless effort
to save the world
from coronavirus
Donald Trump
has proclaimed he's taking
daily doses of
the anti-malaria drug
hydroxychloroquine
with potentially serious
side effects
including instant death
as a nice little chaser
just before his morning pint
of disinfectant

give this man
the Nobel Prize for Medicine
RIGHT NOW!

I'm sure he could
also be convinced
that cyanide is
a cure for arthritis
or paraquat is
a cure for the common cold
and to add them immediately
to his bathroom cabinet
of suicidal refreshment

the reflecting plaque says
Jim and Betty Gillespie
who died in 2007
and 2019 respectively

Together in Barshaw Park
where their love
began to blossom

but you're not allowed to sit
on their black dedicated bench
at the top of Barshaw Park hill
in case a sudden swarm
of Paisley locusts
descends with
the same idea

elbowing for bench space
watching out
for the bench police

you can stand if you want
amongst the bottle tops
and cigarette ends

look at distant clouds
over memorised lochs

just don't touch anyone
or anything
be perfectly inhuman
for the rest of forever

even the ghosts
have to social distance

leaning against the trig point
on the summit of golf course ridge
I can see in the east
the death star hospital
University tower
the science centre
the squinty bridge

armadillo
glinting in the sun

buildings on a far-off planet
non-lockdown cars
in their proper lanes

in the west
the Town Hall clock
observatory dome
the Chinese pagoda flats
on Montgomery Road

a handicapped golfer
hacking at an orange ball

a black-grey raggle-taggle dog
wanders up and growls
and bares its teeth

it turns and goes
then comes back and growls
and bares its teeth

I can tell that it hates me

its young-girl owner
says *Sorry!* and tells *Rolo* off
Bad Rolo!
Don't do that Rolo!

I can tell that she hates me

the blue paper and card bins
are already stuffed to the brim
with paper and card and there
are two weeks until their turn
to be emptied

this didn't use to happen
the world was regular
as clockwork

people must be ordering
lots of comforting stuff
from assorted sources
and having it delivered
when previously
in ancient times
the paper and card waste
would have been more
efficiently distributed
over sensible bin locations
in the Central Belt
and the unevenness
would never have arisen

this didn't use to happen
the world was clockwork
as regular

I shall certainly pad down
when it's dark and go through
the bins to find out who
the major offenders are
for my own information
my own conclusions

create a log of names and times
sizes and stamps

this didn't happen
the world was

it's high pressure
we're on the grass

a Tesco one-click van arrives
with crate after crate
of fuck knows what
for our neighbours
on the highest floor

he asks if there's a lift
and we say no

we point
to the top

as he ascends
into shadow
I wonder why they're getting
such a huge delivery
as they're all fit
have a car
could easily
get it themselves
and none of them
can be self-isolating
as one of them
is outside sunbathing
and they're not scared
as far as I can deduce

getting red
and redder

solar meat

there must be an explanation
the paranoia must be obeyed
you can think about things
too much
too much

it’s sunny
that’s enough

we’re all on the grass
the lunatics are on the grass

a black rove beetle
with a Latin name
falls from the plum tree
above my head

lands on the pages
of my open book

Strange News from Another Star
by Hermann Hesse

I watch it for a bit
christen him 'Kafka'
ping him into outer space

goodbye and good luck
little Franz

there's a big finger out there
waiting to ping me
as well

when I get back in
after being out
I normally don't close the door
entirely
but leave it in
a semi-shut position
so I can
wash my hands right away
in order to remove
all lethal traces of virus
and then go back
once my hands are dried
and close it securely
to keep out disease

there's sadness
in my method

most of the time
I forget
to go back
and put the kettle on
instead
and the door lies extremely
ever-so-slightly open
for ten minutes or
half an hour or
even a whole evening
on one unmemorable occasion

already
erased

due to my
well-intentioned tactical antics
any number
of local impious miscreants
could sneak up the stairs
into the flat
coughing and grogging
and sneezing and belching

urinating on the lampshade
excreting on the flooring
very
quietly
tiptoe out again
satisfied and saying *Ha Ha*
you're going to catch Covid-19
you sarky poetic know-all
and one day they probably will

at the window for
the weekly cacophony

checking to see
who else is at
their position of choice
window or door
driveway or lawn

so and so
so and so
people not at
their usual spot

maybe they've
had enough

the temptation
to say *fuck it*
was too much

will we clap tonight
or batter a lid
wallop a pan?

the next world is ours
it's live on TV

as lockdown metamorphoses
will the Thursday thank you
imperceptibly melt away
getting quieter each week
until there's just
one lone clanger
like a piper on
the battlements

flowers of the forest
incremental resumption
of Life as we want it

Do you mind the days
when we'd stand
at our windows
and hit a pot?
Let everyone else know
that everyone is still here

Christ
it seems so long ago

a deep inescapable note
like the message
of a November bell

three hundred
and sixty-three dead
yesterday

a father wearing
a black cagoule
and a grey pair of long shorts

is giving his daughter
a coalie-back
on the field in the rain

three hundred
and fifty-one dead
tomorrow

and tomorrow
and tomorrow

evil aide Dominic Cummings
ignores the lockdown rules
and drives to Durham
infected with arrogance

sinister sphincter-
licker Michael Gove
slimes to his defence and says
caring for your wife and child
is not a crime
even though
Cummings
could easily have found
someone else in London
to look after the boy
even though
if anyone else had tried it
and driven 250 miles
they would have been
turned back and pounced on
as a prime example
of anti-social behaviour
by politicians eager for blood
and custodial sentences
even though
people have had to let
the ones they love die alone
and be buried alone
because it was classed as a crime
if they broke the rules
but it's okay for Cummings
to follow his 'instinct'

the tiny puppets understand
they cannot dance
without the puppeteer

with rain coming down
a siren from some dream
I think
I'll look at
a video on YouTube
of a funny talking dog
I haven't seen in ages years
probably years
probably years
with the nasty master
going on about maple bacon
and beef in the fridge
giving treats to the cat
the dog
whining because
there's nothing
there's nothing
with its big face up
against a camera but
the sound on the speakers
keeps crackling and stopping
and coming back on
and it's impossible to
enjoy it anymore with
the rain coming down
the master unseen like
some unhinged bastard god

things to do
to amuse yourselves with
in bed during lockdown

1.
Read the paper
2.
Do a crossword
3.
Invent a brief
extremely non pc history
of the now extinct
very smelly band of Native Americans
called the Big Guff tribe
led by Chief StinkBum HonkNiff
(known to his pals as Dances With Turds)
who were finally defeated
at the infamous Reek Creek Massacre
carried out by their arch-enemies
the ScroteScratch led by Chief Shitting Bull
(known to his pals as Crazy Arse)
which is quite close to
the Ohwattapong Mountains
and Guffalo Springs
over which the city of Stenchburg
was founded now twinned with Mingsville
4.
Have sex

almost time to put on
the BBC round-the-clock news again
channel 231

another chance to stare up
the dark sneezy noseholes
of some wide-faced moonhead
in their spare bedroom
with shelves of books
about dead politicians
in the background
as they babble on
about the latest balloon
to botch things up

I can hardly wait
it's the high spot of the day

as I piss into the toilet
a delicate house moth
I had noticed
earlier in the day
flies out fast from
under the rim of the bowl
but gets caught
in the stream
and plummets
into the gathering froth

terrifying maelstrom

I finish and look
a bit closer and can see it
fluttering a bit
dying in the pish
I pull the plug
with a heavy heart
try to banish it
out of my mind

I look ten minutes later
and its body
is still there

if I had the time again
I would reach down
and dip my hand
into my own wee-wee
scoop it clear
of the golden pool
let it dry its wings
in the sun
like some
benevolent god but
I didn't and went and
wrote a poem instead

I'm taking a photo
of a social distancing notice
in the grid-armoured window
of Gleddoch Family Butchers
and thinking at the same time

about the distance of society

a car pulls up
a man winds down
his passenger window
and says *Hi Graham*
how are you doin?
Good to see you

I smile and don't know
who it is

I soon establish it's a man
I see most days
striding around
the cricket field
I didn't recognise him
out of context

the connection unmade

he shouldn't exist beyond
the perimeter of the field
dimensions of the grass
dimensions of the nets

the tender emptiness
of green circles

the balance is upset
the nature of society
and the distance it contains

I tell him I don't think
I'll be doing a walk today

CUSTOMER NOTICE
SOCIAL DISTANCING IN PRACTICE

the clocks days weeks
moving so quickly
you would think it would be
the other way

slowly
being

slow

we're almost
at three months
it's getting faster

a phenomenon
phenomenon

strange dance
of the brain
the invention of time

a man-made attempt
to govern our fates

David's been buried
for two and a half weeks

there's too much to do
nowhere to do it

we watch *Jaws* tonight
as it's nearly the 45th Anniversary

the scene
where everyone
runs screaming from the water
and trampling over old people
followed by the closing
of the beaches
gives me a twang of nostalgia
for the magical days
of panic-buying
and total lockdown

'easing of restrictions'
doesn't have the same ring

being bitten in half by a shark
is all you need
to cheer yourself up

hey kids!
come and do
the Great Greenlaw Drive
Lockdown Treasure Hunt!

see if you can find

a super-flat can of *Irn-Bru*
that's been run over so many times
it's visually fused with the road

an empty quarter bottle of *Buckfast*
twinkling in the sun
on a garden wall

a pigeon feather
a blue latex glove
a bottle of *Doctor Pepper*
another blue latex glove

a shopping trolley a long way from home
a Smoking Kills-flavour cigarette packet
a white polystyrene takeaway tray

a brown paper bag
resting peacefully in the shade
of an all-seeing urban tree

its work done

the winner gets to have
a virtual hug from your granny
on the other side
of a pane of glass

a social distance stretched out line
of three exercisers
including myself
on the dark path alongside
the old maternity hospital
in Barshaw Park

one lone woman passing
the other way
says
I seem to be moving
in the opposite direction
to everyone else

I prattle nonsense in reply

five seconds later I realise
I should have said
That's okay
you're just testing
your eyesight but she's
already gone

tomorrow is
the partial lifting
of lockdown rules
combined with 70 Fahrenheit

NEGLECT AND INJECT
PROTECT AND INSPECT

everyone will be tanking
to Erskine beach
in cars and on bikes

hovercraft and submarines
zeppelins and pogo sticks

pasty supermodels from Paisley
will be glooping on the oil
pulling a ring
installing their thongs

beer-bellied one-pack
lovegods with mullets
will be strutting and preening
displaying their bulge

High Street prima donnas
New Street John Travoltas

ice cream vans
selling heroin and 99s
a return to the norm

raspberry sauce
crumbly flakes

ERECT AND DISSECT
REJECT AND DEFECT

last night the latest space rocket
failed to take off
because of bad cloud

if you’re lucky you’ll see me
launching from the Bridge

I can now go fishing and golfing
and soon I'll be able to resume
all my favourite activities
and do a few I haven't done before
as they say you should try
everything once
before you die
such as
extreme ironing
extreme breathing
extreme tea drinking
extreme taxidermy
clog dancing
bog dancing
cock fighting
sock fighting
hedgehog boxing
sloth stretching
seal clubbing
lizard painting
ant baiting
platypus throwing
pubic hair trimming
dancing with hamsters
astronomy with wasps
mathematics with bees
witch burning
watch turning
lunatic taunting
frog squirting
cow squeezing
sheep worrying
sheep hugging
tree shagging
mouse trimming
hedge trimming
pole dancing
hole dancing
extreme genocide
extreme self-medication
parachuting with penguins

target practice with politicians
swimming with pangolins
canoeing with baboons
bat scoffing
time wasting

a meat wagon in Barshaw
is hoovering up
sunstroked dissenters
in the skew-whiff land
of my febrile bonce

chomping at the bit
for an instinct-crime arrest

it isn't real
it's just like pictures
in a book

I smile at two bobbies
young enough to be
my grandkids if
I'd had a kid to begin with
as they plod past in the park

a ginger girl
black-hair boy

I flirt with the idea
of telling them
there are 40 swans
on the sparkling pond
with no understanding
of the concept
of social distance
but they'd cuff me
for silly insolence
avian disrespect

they smile back
but I know they know

if this was America
they'd kneel on my neck

sounds in the distance
sounds like someone
giving a free concert
from their front lawn

out of tune crooning
drifting on the wind

lost chords
muffed beats

later the sound of
Elton John singing
'Tiny Dancer'

blue-jean baby
has got the rabies
or something like that

maybe he's flown in
on his private jet
to resuscitate
the Buddies of Paisley
raise money
for the NHS

'Rocket Man' and 'Your Song'
from a flappy marquee
a soft auditorium
in Abbey Close

madman specs
transplanted hair

geez Kroakodile Rock
ya big poof!

or maybe it's just
an old-fashioned tape
someone found in a box
and pressed PLAY

manual over-ride
a reminder of a clunkier age
lighter air

L.A. Lady
likes onion gravy
or something like that

madmen across the water

Trump in his bunker
America burning

he says he'll
send in the military
with their tanks
rockets and B52s

deploy the space force

nuke them from orbit
just to be sure
gas the crowds
for a photo op

bible in his hand
bedlam in his head

a drone filming
a forest of phones
filming a funeral

recording ourselves

when they vote him back in
their land is damned

people lost

moron convoys
are snaking to Luss
for a day of booze
discovering fire

the ungraspables
the ones who cannot grasp
that something exists
outside of their cars

huddling in sunshine
pissing against walls
defecating behind trees

sexual excitement
aeons of excrement
stinking in the heat

ungrown children
clad in skins
queuing for meat
at the drive-thru altar

praying to nothingness
addicted to death

the beasts are loose
the hopeless heads
of primeval impulse

black blankness
lord of the void

people are scared
of themselves

the water on the Loch
is always beautiful
something good
will always happen

the second wave
will soon be here

carry us back
to before
the beginning

as I step up to the strip
at the hand basket till
in Marks and Spencer
on the 8th of June
an old woman
in the aisle to my left says
EXCUSE ME
EXCUSE ME
THERE'S A QUEUE
THERE'S A QUEUE!

I say sorry
smile
retreat
think to myself
'yes there's a queue
and you're standing
in the wrong one
for the big trolleys so
MAKE SURE YOU STAND
IN THE PROPER QUEUE
YOU OLD FUCKING BAG!'

give me an enemy I can see
instead of thin air

five minutes on
I pass her outside the door
lighting-up an already
half-dragged fag in her gob
consider roaring
into her face
EXCUSE ME
EXCUSE ME
THERE'S NO CURE
THERE'S NO CURE!
but keep on walking
down to Dunn Square

a man is talking into his phone
at Queen Victoria's feet

a mask on his chin

the Town Hall clock
bongs half past ten
the river still flows
but the spirits sink

the well of compassion
hath finally run dry

returning from our
cricket field walk
we see a magpie being
chased by another
slam into the front door
of our flats

the hard glass
a hard sound

it's out for the count
as the other pecks
at its eye

deep in the nest of
feathered subconscious

it hasn't a scooby
where or what it is
completely bamboozled

the same as us
without a clue

we wait with it
for twenty minutes
coax it back
onto its feet

we call him Maurice

we can't go up
we feel responsible
if we leave him alone
he hasn't a chance

marmalized
cannibalized

he finally flies
into the trees

we'll never see him again

the well of compassion
hath replenished itself

at least as far
as birds are concerned

at *The Car Park In The Sky*
at the top of the Braes
four miles there
four miles back

a volcanic plateau
of Clyde lava

if I could look through the rock
I could see all the way
to the Earth's core
a clenched ball of angry fire

there's not much here
a bin
a view
a man with a dog called Laika
named after
the first dog
to die in space

it's usually heaving
with loved-up smoochers
hormonal heavy-petters
capitulation
copulation
impregnation

but there's only
a solitary steamed-up Astra
with a YES sticker
on the back window

a self-isolator
spanking the monkey

I can see lots of things
but the distance makes
perspectives compress
geologies melt
geometries unfold

Abbey
churches
beerless pubs
lined-up boneyard airport planes

if I could look through buildings
I could see all the way
to the house where I live
through the window
onto the couch

me and Helen
sitting there watching
Journey to the Centre of the Earth

on the way down
I'm singing the song
'Trampolene' spelt with an e
by Julian Cope
when I spookily
glance to my left
from the high path
and there's
a blue trampoline spelt with an i
in a tiny back garden
far below

well I stand at heaven's gate
come see me cry
heaven's gate is locked
they will not let me by

the cosmic tumblers
bounce into place

further on the way down
I see Delbert Grady
wearing knee-length grey shorts
and pushing a pink pram
up Caplethill Road

he's the baldy bowtie waiter
in *The Shining*
who tells Jack
to murder Wendy and Danny
and calls Hallorann 'a nigger'

not very nice at all

it's definitely him
I'm not hallucinating
through sheer exhaustion

which worryingly means
that Caplethill Road
must be either
a safe-haven-bolthole
a bit like Argentina
for racist phantoms
or a portal to
an evil dimension

it's all becoming clear

a gust of wind
blows the packet of crisps
from my hand
and scatters what's left
on the grass

even further on the way down
I pass the white-haired man
with a paintbrush
in his right hand
who's still painting
the black fence
he was painting 3 hours ago
when I passed him
for the first time

I suddenly remember reading
that when Robert Burns
wasn’t shagging women
he had ambitions to become
a slave-driver-overseer
in a sugar plantation
to make a lot of easy cash
on the misery of others
but chickened out
at the last minute
and stuck to shagging instead

and in one of his poems
he had a good laugh
slagging off some
prominent abolitionists

A Man’s A Man For A’ That
unless he’s black

eh Rab?

I can’t remember
the name of the poem
or the abolitionists

I suppose this means
for the sake of consistency
they’ll have to tear down
all of his statues
and rename the 25th of January
‘Burn the Black Man Night’

they’re rioting on TV
and posting again
with lots of followers
smiles and hearts

Black Lives Matter activists
versus right-inclined bootboys
and all of them
versus the police

spraying stuff
on assorted statues
of politicians and slave traders
past and present
loved and loathed

Paddington Bear is next
followed by Peter Pan
and I’ve never liked
George Orwell’s hair

the ‘don’t mention the war’
episode of *Fawlty Towers*
is now classed alongside
the gas chambers
of Auschwitz
as crimes against humanity

the law of England
nothing to do with me

outside our window
Mister Softy
is chiming
‘I Wish I Was In Dixie’

I’ve started using the word *pie*
instead of the real word
or part of the word
when I’m setting up
a recording of a film
on the DVD player

today I set up a recording
of the old 1947 version
of *Nicholas Nickleby*
but typed in *Nicholas Nicklepie*
instead

it gives it a real feeling
of dignified authenticity
to see it up on the screen

Psycho
would become *Piecho*
Lord of the Flies
would become *Lord of the Pies*
Twelve Angry Men
would become *Twelve Angry Pies*

if there was a film version
of *The Catcher in the Rye*
I’d call it *The Catcher in the Pie*
or even *The Pie in the Rye*
but there isn’t

I think I’ll target books next
stick the word pie
over the titles on the spines
Nineteen Eighty-Pie
Wuthering Pies
Pie of Darkness
Frankenpie
Pie and Punishment
Three Pies in a Boat
The Pie and the Fury
Moby Pie

Steppenpie
One Hundred Pies of Solitude

some just wouldn't work at all
Pieysses and *The Pieal*
sound ridiculous
and *Pie the Obscure*
doesn't make sense

sometimes it just feels right
to contort the truth
to suit my own agenda

the world I think
the world
should be

this could go on forever
but I'll draw a line
at *Brave New Pie*
and *The Pie of Miss Jean Brodie*

Tuesday is
Chinese din-dins day

I buy it in
Marks and Spencer
every week
on the same day
following Sunday
the name of which
I've forgotten

egg fried rice
beef and black bean
crispy lemon chicken

The Gang of Three

the employee behind
a spit-proof screen

most of the time
the boxes are on the shelves
but sometimes they aren't
I search and search
but there's no
crispy lemon chicken
and nothing else will do

I go through the phases
starting with
mild irritation
then anger
shaking
crying
and finally curling up
in a womb-baby position
sucking my thumb

it's that caramelised sugar
and gelling agent
that holds us together

makes corona worthwhile

leads us through
the darkest hours

all the way
from the virus markets
a yummy cycle
of gluten and death

we're all alive
eight hours before we die
someone says
on a DVD
we're watching as we
eat our tea

Nordic Noir

we're all alive
eight hours before we die

not seven
or nine or six
or ten

I think to myself
'that is a great line
I'll have to use it
in a poem someday'

about existence
the perception
the existence

of perception

inclusive
consciousness

or was it
everyone's alive
eight hours before they die?

I'll have to go back
to the start
if I want to be sure

everyone's alive
eight hours before they die

I thought to myself
'that was a great line
I've used it
in a poem someday'

as I gaze again
at the cricket field
I wonder if one morning
I'll gaze and see
a giraffe grazing
on the succulent grass

sticking its neck into
the indigenous trees
having a skwatch
in the garden sheds

it would certainly
be different

it heard about
the rich pickings
at the Kelburne Cricket Club
on the internet
and flew out giraffe class
on Serengeti Airlines
with a hole cut in the roof
for its head

two weeks in quarantine
then onto the pitch
with all of his pals

dogs crows
flies bees
the endangered laughing
Scottish hyena

it could happen
there is still time

I wonder about this for a while
then wonder about
something else

on our second circuit
passing familiar twigs

we discuss the resurgence
of the virus in China
and then
try to think up names
for toiletries and
personal grooming products
that monsters from
the horror films would use
such as
Frankenfresh feminine wipes
Mrs. Snatcher's dead body wash
Decapitated Head and Shoulders

also
Quasimodo's Sanctuary Spa Giftset
Phantom of the Opera Pamper Set
Igor's beeswax beard-balm and brush
Beast With Five Fingers manicure set
Mr Hyde's nasal trimmer
Nosferatu's fang-flossing kit
(with optional whitening powder
and strips)

maybe even
Count Dracula's shaving mirror
Mrs. Dracula's *Vamoose!* coffin spray
The Wolfman's *Bad Moon* hair gel
Im-Ho-Tep's moisturiser for dry skin
King Kong's jungle-fresh conditioner
The Undead-friendly portable exfoliator
(also suitable for zombies)

and last but least
GILLETTE! THE BEST
A GHOUL CAN GET!
to be sung to the same tune
as the well-known advert

on our third circuit
passing familiar twigs ....

beside a tabloid photo
of a woman arriving
at a Scottish airport
is printed the caption
NEW NOMRAL
instead of
NEW NORMAL

a sloppy mistype
from an isolated captioneer
tired of fingering
his keyboard all day

NOMRAL
(*sounds a bit like*
a drug)
is the name
they could give
to the elusive vaccine
when they eventually find it

everyone will be
queuing round the block
to get their dose of NOMRAL
from the doctor

everyone will be
buying packets of NOMRAL
from the chemist
along with their deodorant
and flavoured condoms

NOMRAL
will save the world
from capitalist miniaturisation

NOMRAL
will bring love
NOMRAL
will bring prosperity
NOMRAL

will guarantee satisfaction
NOMRAL
will make everybody the same

NOMRAL
will bring back
some nomrality to our lives

the Government have announced
that from this exact moment

you can hug
your third youngest grandchild
for half an hour each day
but only if your middle name is Ebenezer

you can have your hair cut
as long as you don't have any hair

you can have your throat cut
as long as you don't have any throat

you can meet up
with a family of your choice
but not at the same time
and not in the same place

you can play scrabble in the morning
and sing opera in the afternoon
with your first cousin twice removed
but only if they were born
in Auchtermuchty at 6 a.m.

you can have sex twice a month
with your last cousin eight times removed

you can have sex five times a day
with a complete stranger as long as
you stay two metres apart

you can wear your underpants
outside of your trousers three times a day
as long as you can prove
you have a womb

you can stand in a bookshop
and drink a carry out
but you can't go into a pub
and read a book

you can go into a hairdresser
as long as you go in upside down
while singing 'Flower of Scotland'
and wearing a Sturgeon-
shaped messiah mask

our fellow resident Albert
the potted-plant-pirate
the washable-flower-buccaneer
is at the front door of the flats
holding it open
with his arm barring the way
which means I'll have to
go close
to get out
but I craftily use my foot
to take the door's weight
and dodge out

untouched
in space
in Tesco

as an afterthought
on a summer day
I buy an unhealthy
global warming-plastic box
of blueberries which
proceeds to burst open
as the check-out lad
is scanning
spilling
healthy fruit
all over the conveyor belt
and someone has to fetch another
from the farthest side of

the galaxy
the shop
the bus

passes
with an old couple on board
sitting smiling on a happy trip
into town but they're not
wearing facemasks which
is currently compulsory

I get home
check
the newspaper to find
you're not ordered to wear a mask
until Monday but that's no excuse
they should be reported
to the police and shot against
a wall and so should I as
I reckon I've had
enough

our 14th wedding anniversary
is on the horizon
fast approaching

I order a tasteful
Pandemic Anniversary card
from tax-avoiding Amazon

a personalised date
optionally included

but if I want I could also buy
a quarantine T-shirt
with multi-coloured lines
like the London underground
and words like
couch fridge window etc.
instead of the names of stations

a lockdown photo frame
with a cartoon of Boris Johnson
and The Simpsons
wearing facemasks on it

or even
a QUARANTINE mug
with a friendly cartoon coronavirus on it
an I SURVIVED CORONAVIRUS mug
a BORED AS FUCK adult colouring book
a WHERE'S THE FUCKING TOILET PAPER?
adult colouring book
a CORONAVIRUS 2020 I WAS THERE T-shirt
a STRAIGHT OUTTA ISOLATION
a STRAIGHT OUTTA SANITISER
a STRAIGHT OUTTA WUHAN lady's vest
and last but not least
a FUCK YOU CORONA! T-shirt
for men/women/children

select your size

no customer reviews
as yet

the last teatime briefing
the last televisual feast

lecterns and microphones
beginning to gather dust

giant zoom-face screens
unplugged at the wall

the last time we'll have to
turn over fast
to *Pointless*

'we asked one hundred people
to name a country with
a higher per capita death rate
than Britain'

there are none
to choose from

the Crime Minister
turning and fading into history
like John Wayne
at the end of *The Searchers*

in need of
a haircut

a trail of bodies
in his wake

I subconsciously misread
the ever-changing caption
across the bottom
of the BBC News Channel
and think it says
Sheep reopen in Wales
instead of
Shops reopen in Wales

I can see vast traffic jams
on the Severn Bridge
as bestiality fans
with Cockney accents
invade the valleys
to take advantage of
the newly opened sheep
at user-friendly prices

it's a mind-mistake
anyone could make
when they've been denied
compliant ruminant company
and intellectual discussion
of the political fable
Animal Farm
for three bloody months

a nan-gran
on the cricket grass

teaching her
blonde granddaughter
to march in step

a future soldier
in a pinky top

left right left right
swing those arms

a pyramid
of long pine cones
waiting to be
put in a sack

casualties for
the bonfires
of lockdown

attention salute
fall in fall out

today I walk to Ralston
where I no longer live

there are lots of rainbows
in the windows
and the porches

the affluent inhabitants
obviously have
remarkable access
to crayons and paper
blue tack and tape

THANK YOU NHS
WASH YOUR HANDS
SWEET ISOLATION
I HAVE HOPE

one expressionist brammer
looks like a scene from hell
a deconstructed spectral splat

there's nothing in
the window of 55

what's the name
for a crowd of rainbows?

there's a silver
teardrop-shaped Christmas bauble
like a sci-fi spaceship's torpedo
lying in the gutter
on Atholl Cescent

there's no reason for it
to be here except
to be found by me

I put it in my pocket
save it for later

a coughing postman
delivers a box

a woman opens
and takes it in

small footsteps following me
turn out to be a leaf
dancing along with the wind

I put it in my pocket
save it for later

HANK YOU
ALL KEY WORKERS
on a sheet of card
on a bungalow's door

a single red rose
stuck in the keyhole
of a water mains plate

perhaps
in remembrance
of the missing T

a crow couple close together
on the railing at the top
of the pavilion steps

I go to where
I used to play headers with Des
at the far side of the playing fields

now an overgrown sea
of dock leaves
swaying daisies on elegant necks

I skim my hand
along the tops of the knee-high grass
like Russell Crowe in *Gladiator*

a wild garden
the doorway to Elysium

at the back of the school
there's a drawing in a window
of a sleeping child
cradled in the curve
of a crescent moon
next to the message
we need
to know

Ralston Primary
is a NUT FREE school

a greenfly lands
on the left-eye lens of my glasses
jumps before I can
blow it away

a razzmatazz of rainbows

strong weeds are striving
through the tarmac cracks
behind the primary school spikes

a *trypraying.co.uk* banner
is outside the church
where David Tennant's father
used to be minister

a consolation of rainbows

a cat on a sill
looking into a tree
at something it sees

relative dimensions
in time or space

a rainbow parliament

a black skull and crossbones flag
flapping on a sloping lawn

the library where
I once borrowed
The Invisible Man is shut

a scrunched-up facemask
lying on Buchlyvie Road

melancholy drawings
of a woman and man
on a double-glazed dormer

STAY SAFE
fading in the Junelight

this is where
my dead mum's dead uncle Hugh
used to live

he sailed the seven seas
had a girl in every port

whenever I passed
he would press a pound coin
into my hand and ask me
How's your love life?

even when I was
thirty years old

I would tell him
the melancholy answer

this is the place to come
if you need some cash

the safety of the past

a red telephone box
and a blue police call box
at the back of a back garden
on Strathmore Avenue

this is the place to come
if you need some help

soon the sewers
will be clogged
with maskbergs

coagulations
of polyester
stuffed down the pan
to join
the masses
of grease and fat
earplugs and wipes

lava-soap growths
the size of a bus
another landmark
of human delight

the world has learnt
to wash its hands

there’s a woman
in the doorway of Greggs
with a tattoo on her arm
and a visor on her head

touting for business
before they go bust

hello dearie
fancy a freshly-made
egg and cress baguette?

my sky
is grey

I don’t think I’ll bother
disinfecting
the shopping today

looking in the mirror
snipping at my reflection
with a pair of scissors

trying not to
look in my eyes

look at my skin
look at my scars

of laughter
or strain

I can feel the hair
falling to the floor

is it the right hairs
or the wrong hairs?

it's hard to co-ordinate
untangle
in what direction
I should be moving my hand

brain tells me one thing
mirror tells me another

towards
or away

there's a cut on my forehead
where a bin lid thumped
as I was dumping
the newspapers
for the morning lorry

latest rubbish
the headline collection

it's in almost exactly
the same place where

the garage door got me

a few long
weeks ago

I’m the wrong way round
this world is front to back

a snapping Chihuahua
with hunger
for blood

scurries
past a can
of *Blue Charge* energy drink
creatively placed
in the black-hole-neck
of a mutilated traffic cone

plonked on top
of an electrical box

a Turner Prize exhibit

across the road
from a two litre
three-quarter-full container
of green lid semi-skimmed milk
sitting outside a driveway's gate

a stockpile castoff
corona orphan

the gift of life
for a passing stranger

blood in my shit
there it is

oh well
probably just
a pile

a pile of smiles
a smile of piles

if Covid-19
doesn’t get you
then something
else will

the Three Wise Men
of Barshaw Central
are sprucing up
the miniature railway
in anticipation of
the summer-Stalag-
liberation rush

one man beneath a hat
is excitedly slapping
corona-repellent green paint
onto the wooden supports
of the circular track

a second man with
a sploshy container
is spraying a piss-width stream
of killer liquid
onto the weeds
in the junction concrete

the third man appears
to be painting
the leaves of the trees
but on closer inspection
is actually talking
on his mobile phone

perhaps he's asking
a fourth man
who's standing
in the shadows
of the branches
what colour they should be

the upturned wooden tables
opposite the Rowantree Café
in Barshaw Park
emanate a vibe
of don't-come-near-me
patient
menace

KEEP AWAY
BUGGER OFF

what used to be
an exalted spot
for a cheeseburger picnic
now looks like
the scary anti-tank defences
the Nazis placed
on the Normandy beaches

Czech Hedgehogs
HISTORIC SITE

in 100 years time
they'll create
an Archaeological Protectorate
full of replica tables
in a fenced-off hectare
including real un-mown grass
a couple of rare plastic bottles
the same old fountain
a random scatter
of black bags full of dog shite
and name it
CORONAWORLD

talking educational holograms
of Johnson and Sturgeon
Hancock and Raab

the heads of experts
no one remembers

people will come
to ooh and aah
point and laugh
and sanitise their hands
with guides in period costume
and racks of clothes
including PPE
Jacob Rees-Mogg three-piece suits
Dominic Cummings beanie hats
for children to try on
and look in the mirror
and take selfies just
by blinking their eyes

re-enactors teaching
the art of isolation
avoiding questions
on the poetry of quarantine

A PERFECT DAY OUT
FOR ALL THE FAMILY

finished nicely
with a browse in the shop
for a STAY ALERT fridge magnet
or a SAVE LIVES tea towel
and a bargain bin copy
of CORONAWORLD
by Graham Fulton
FREE with every purchase

alternatively
a more likely scenario
is we'll have
blown ourselves up by then
with our old chum the atomic bomb
who's been forgotten about
during the pandemic

half the survivors
will take refuge
in the basements
of unused hospitals
where over time
their skin will turn
the same colour of blue
as the common-or-garden
disposable facemask
and their hair
will become
a long messy albino
a bit like
an embarrassing politician
from the crumbling books
on the library shelves

they'll be known
as Borlocks

the other half
will try to subsist
on the surface
by consuming vast quantities
of Salt and Vinegar crisps
and *FUDCO* cashews

they'll be known
as Snowflakes

every Thursday night
the hungry Borlocks
will pound their pots and pans

to summon the sappy Snowflakes
who'll walk passively
to the abattoir
with happy glassy eyes
while chanting
PROTECT THE NHS
over and over

I vowed
I would
never do
an elbow bump
but today I did
an elbow bump

it happened
was over
before I
knew it

my cousin
coming out
of Tesco

I did it
without question
I was only
following orders

from my rusty-
machinery brain

I was an
elbow bump virgin
but now I'm
an elbow bump hoor

a surrender monkey
to the system

a brown round coin
on the pavement
in Clarence Street

I bend down to pick up
the last 2p
on Earth

put it in the line
above the fireplace
with all the rest

a solar system of discs
the Covid Hoard

the currency
of coronaworld
is no longer
legal tender

the bank
is closed

everyone
has flown

no need to fret

it will open again
someday soon

at a right time

we put the coins into
a pretty little filigree box
we bought in a Souk
in Tripoli

I make a tiny scroll
with the words
The Covid Hoard
written in my
fanciest script

there's not enough room
for all of them
for everything

some have to
remain outside

histories have to
be left behind

others keep on
appearing

is if they're
trying to tell us
it isn't allowed
to be done just yet

30-06-2020
11:07
Hi Jim. I haven't heard from you for a while. I've been keeping busy. I'll try and get through in the near future for a proper catch up.
I hope all is well.
Let me know. Bye.

the field is empty
except for us

no keep-fitters
circuit walkers
no lollop or dollop
pom-pom or chico

they're all away
to the English pubs

we decide to have
a game of putting
using Helen's stick
as a club

a leaf as a tee
a scrape of mud
or a scrap of litter
as a hole or cup

a fallen crab-apple
as a ball

Isaac Newton's
Adam and Eve's
science or religion
reason or faith

find what you need
to take you through

Helen's cooking with gas
sinking putt after putt
but I'm unable to judge
the distance
and weight
curve of the planet

it always ends up
too short

a lifetime from where
it ought to be

I convert the apple
into the trees
with the toe of my shoe

when we’re ready to go

www.ingramcontent.com/pod-product-compliance
Lightning Source LLC
Chambersburg PA
CBHW040925190426
43197CB00032B/1
* 9 7 8 1 9 1 3 1 4 4 1 9 7 *